Ferguson

Man Vs

The law

ISBN-13:
978-1516846351

ISBN-10:
1516846354

Fergusons' Origin

Ferguson was founded in 1855 when William B. Ferguson deeded 10 acres (4.0 ha) of land to the *Wabash Railroad* in exchange for a new depot and naming rights.

The settlement that sprang up around the depot was called Ferguson Station. Ferguson was the first outside station connected to *St. Louis*.

The station is a focal point of the city's history and is depicted on the city flag, designed in 1994.

Ferguson's first schoolhouse was built in 1878. Ferguson was incorporated as a city in 1894.

Emerson Electric moved its headquarters to Ferguson during the 20th century.

According to the Census report of 2013; Ferguson has 29.3% whites and 67.4%

blacks in this community. The population since 2010 has grown to over 20,000.

Periodically; small towns will develop their own rules and policies and impose them on those whom they feel that are unlearned.

This is why each and all citizens should acclimate themselves to their own government laws on what they mean in regards to them as a citizen.

What can cripple some is that they fail to read, educate, share, listen, or gather important information which is essential for their daily living.

The scriptures states in Hosea 4:5 that; "My people are destroyed for the lack of knowledge." We all should find ways to keeps ourselves abreast to daily and global news. This isn't for the African Americans, but for all Americans.

I know of persons whom don't watch the television. They have a fear of listening to bad news from the media.

In my opinion this will keep some glued to their own morals. We must face challenges whether we desire to view them or experience them.

We are owners of several non profit organizations. One of our elements provides tools, and training for entrepreneurs and non entrepreneurs for business.

I felt this is a must in the United States. We train those to remove themselves from the old way of thinking to; "I know I can."

Our organization supports all races and backgrounds whom desire to achieve higher goals.

But it will begin first in our mindset. We must learn how to become more effective in our own country.

The era in Ferguson is just a piece of the pie of not getting the full understanding of a matter. We have never lost a child due to gun violence or any other death.

However; we do respect the families whom have lost children or loved ones due to any sort of violence or alleged injustice.

Many have stated that the town or city of Ferguson has always practiced prejudice and racism for years.

How can we define this? You would need to be a citizen in this town in order to answer this.

Many times their will be those whom react from impulse and not their thoughts. They will react out of fear and not conscious.

There will be accidents which will occur and those whom maybe at fault will deny that they made a mistake.

At times, they will attempt to protect their careers and families. We are all human. If we were up against termination or prosecution; it may surprise others what our responses would be.

We sometimes fail to be truthful in order to protect some things. We have all been in this situation. These are not "little white lies." They are our thoughts and what could happen if we told the truth. We can fabricate some things in order for the truth to lie in the courtroom or situation.

Were their lies told on both sides from the Ferguson alleges murder? I think there were lies told from both law enforcement and the witnesses whom reported the shooting.

We must remember that what we say can affect others for a life time. We can sentence some to a life term in incarceration or we can discredit someone's character.

Race shouldn't bear any withholdings on the truth. With Ferguson; we have witnessed and heard of law enforcement covering up their faults and actions to unjustified shootings.

We have also heard false statements and testimonies of witnesses to support those due to their race.

As I watched and followed this heartrending contention; I began to learn that we as a people must first learn how to listen and then react. We all have fell short of this issue.

According to James 1:19 & 20 states; "Beloved, let every man be swift to hear, slow to speak, slow to wrath; for the wrath of man worketh not the righteousness of God."

It can be challenging at times to follow one of the golden rules of the Bible. Our adrenaline will react quicker than our thoughts. It's our nature. We must be humbled in this area to develop in this area.

I am learning to overcome many things which will allow me to work out the process in my thoughts first.

The Confederate Flag

The symbolism of the flag is simple and straightforward: It represents the Confederate side in the war that you enjoy studying.

More than likely, your knowledge of the flag has expanded and become more sophisticated over the years. At some point, you learned that the Confederate battle flag was not, in fact, "the Confederate flag" and was not known as the "Stars and Bars."

That name properly belongs to the first national flag of the Confederacy. If you studied the war in the Western and Trans-Mississippi theaters, you learned that "Confederate battle flag" is a misnomer.

Many Confederate units served under battle flags that looked nothing like the red flag with the star-studded blue cross.

You may have grown up with more than just an idle knowledge of the flag's association with the Confederacy and its armies, but also with a reverence for the flag because of its association with Confederate ancestors.

 If you didn't, your interest in the war likely brought you into contact with people who have a strong emotional connection with the flag. And, at some point in your life, you became aware that not everyone shared your perception of the Confederate flag.

 If you weren't aware of this before, the unprecedented flurry of events and of public reaction to them that occurred in June 2015 have raised obvious questions that all students of Civil War history must confront: *Why do people have such different and often conflicting perceptions of what the Confederate flag means, and how did those different meanings evolve?*

The flag as we know it was born not as a symbol, but as a very practical banner. The commanders of the Confederate army in Virginia (then known at the Army of the Potomac) sought a distinctive emblem as an alternative to the Confederacy's first national flag—the Stars and Bars—to serve as a battle flag.

The Stars and Bars, which the Confederate Congress had adopted in March 1861 because it resembled the once-beloved Stars and Stripes, proved impractical and even dangerous on the battlefield because of that resemblance.

 That problem was what compelled Confederate commanders to design and employ the vast array of other battle flags used among Confederate forces throughout the war.

Battle flags become totems for the men who serve under them, for their esprit de corps, for their sacrifices. They assume emotional significance for soldiers' families and their descendants. Anyone today hoping to understand why so many Americans consider the flag an object of veneration must understand its status as a memorial to the Confederate soldier.

It is, however, impossible to carve out a kind of symbolic safe zone for the Confederate battle flag as the flag of the soldier because it did not remain exclusively the flag of the soldier.

By the act of the Confederate government, the battle flag's meaning is inextricably intertwined with the Confederacy itself and, thus, with the issues of slavery and states' rights—over which readers of Civil War Times and the American public as a whole engage in spirited and endless debate.

By 1862, many Southern leaders scorned the Stars and Bars for the same reason that had prompted the flag's adoption the year before: it too closely resembled the Stars and Stripes.

As the war intensified and Southerners became Confederates, they weaned themselves from symbols of the old Union and sought a new symbol that spoke to the Confederacy's "confirmed independence."

That symbol was the Confederate battle flag. Historian Gary Gallagher has written persuasively that it was Robert E. Lee's Army of Northern Virginia, not the Confederate government that best embodied Confederate nationalism.

Lee's stunning victories in 1862–63 made his army's battle flag the popular choice as the new national flag. On May

1, 1863, the Confederacy adopted a flag—known colloquially as the Stainless Banner—featuring the ANV battle flag emblazoned on a white field.

For the remainder of the Confederacy's life, the soldiers' flag was also, in effect, the national flag.

If all Confederate flags had been furled once and for all in 1865, they would still be contentious symbols as long as people still argue about the Civil War, its causes and its conduct.

But the Confederate flag did not pass once and for all into the realm of history in 1865. And for that reason, we must examine how it has been used and perceived since then if we wish to understand the reactions that it evokes today.

 The flag never ceased being the flag of the Confederate soldier and still today commands wide respect as a memorial to the Confederate soldier. The history of the flag since 1865 is marked by the accumulation of additional meanings based on additional uses.

Within a decade of the end of the war (even before the end of Reconstruction in 1877), white Southerners began using the Confederate flag as a memorial symbol for fallen heroes.

By the turn of the 20th century, during the so-called "Lost Cause" movement in which white Southerners formed organizations, erected and dedicated monuments, and propagated a Confederate history of the "War Between the States," Confederate flags proliferated in the South's public life.

Far from being suppressed, the Confederate version of history and Confederate symbols became main stream in the postwar South. The Confederate national flags were part of that mainstream, but the battle flag was clearly preeminent. The United Confederate Veterans (UCV) issued a report in 1904 defining the square ANV pattern flag as the Confederate battle flag, effectively writing out of the historical record the wide variety of battle flags under which Confederate soldiers had served.

The efforts of the UCV and the United Daughters of the Confederacy (UDC) to promote that "correct" battle flag pattern over the "incorrect" rectangular pattern (the Army of Tennessee's or the naval jack) were frustrated by the public's demand for rectangular versions that could serve as the Confederate equivalent of the Stars and Stripes.

What is remarkable looking back from the 21st century is that, from the 1870s and into the 1940s, Confederate heritage organizations used the flag widely in their rituals memorializing and celebrating the Confederacy and its heroes, yet managed to maintain effective ownership of the flag and its meaning. The flag was a familiar part of the South's symbolic landscape, but how and where it was used was controlled.

Hints of change were evident by the early 20th century. The battle flag had emerged not only as the most popular symbol of the Confederacy, but also of the South more generally.

By the 1940s, as Southern men mingled more frequently with non-Southerners in the U.S. Armed Forces and met them on the gridiron, they expressed their identity as Southerners with Confederate battle flags.

The flag's appearance in conjunction with Southern collegiate football was auspicious. College campuses are often incubators of cultural change, and they apparently were for the battle flag.

This probably is owed to the Kappa Alpha Order, a Southern fraternity founded at Washington College (now Washington and Lee University) in 1865, when R.E. Lee was its president.

A Confederate memorial organization in its own right, Kappa Alpha was also a fraternity and introduced Confederate symbols into collegiate life.

It was in the hands of students that the flag burst onto the political scene in 1948. Student delegates from Southern colleges and universities waved battle flags on the floor of the Southern States Rights Party convention in July 1948.

The so-called "Dixie crat" Party formed in protest to the Democratic Party convention's adoption of a civil rights plank. The Confederate flag became a symbol of protest against civil rights and in support of Jim Crow segregation. It also became the object of a high-profile, youth-driven nationwide phenomenon that the media dubbed the "flag fad." Many pundits suspected that underlying the fad was a lingering "Dixie crat" sentiment.

African-American news-papers decried the flag's unprecedented popularity within the Armed Forces as a source of dangerous division at a time when America needed to be united against Communism.

But most observers concluded that the flag fad was another manifestation of youth-driven material culture. Confederate heritage organizations correctly perceived the Dixie crat movement and the flag fad as a profound threat to their ownership of the Confederate flag.

The UDC in November 1948 condemned use of the flag "in certain demonstrations of college groups and some political groups" and launched a formal effort to protect the flag from "misuse."

Several Southern states subsequently passed laws to punish "desecration" of the Confederate flag. All those efforts proved futile. In the decades after the flag fad, the Confederate flag became, as one Southern editor wrote, "confetti in careless hands."

Instead of being used almost exclusively for memorializing the Confederacy and its soldiers, the flag became fodder for beach towels, t-shirts, bikinis, diapers and baubles of every description.

While the UDC continued to condemn the proliferation of such kitsch, it became so commonplace that, over time, others subtly changed their definition of "protecting" the flag to defending the right to wear and display the very items that they once defined as desecration.

As the dam burst on Confederate flag material culture and heritage groups lost control of the flag, it acquired a new identity as a symbol of "rebellion" divorced from the historical context of the Confederacy.

Truckers, motorcycle riders and "good old' boys" (most famously depicted in the popular television show (The Dukes of Hazards) gave the flag a new meaning that transcends the South and even the United States.

So let us conclude this: As some may know and some may not be aware; that when the children of Israel will set up those idol gods; destruction would always take place. Idol gods were and still are a symbol of pride and dominancy.

When we place these statues in our towns, cities, and states which bare no fruit for all and not for some; it can cause much division. The area can begin to experience catastrophic events in their area.

Man will dispute this because they are accustomed to mans' law and not biblical laws and principles from the Bible.

The Confederate flag can be utilized for good from the affects of the war. But we all know that to some it has been utilized as racism of control.

There shouldn't be any any kind of symbol to remind us of anything. The Confederate flags should come down in all states to bring back more unity in our great country.

In one of our Metropolitan areas here in the south; the city decided to bring Ramses to the area as an exhibit.

The area has experienced divided governments, divided school systems, crime, teen violence, and poverty.

I will share with you a little history regarding Ramses.

For over 20 years a huge statue of Egypt's pharaoh-god was dwarfed by the building it stood in front of: America's Largest Pyramid on the outskirts of Memphis, Tennessee.

But the pyramid failed as an attraction and was sold to *Bass Pro Shops*, which planned to turn it into a huge, oddly-shaped store.

With no more need for a protective deity, the pyramid was separated from Ramses II on April 24, 2012, and the city trucked the statue several miles east to the campus of the University of Memphis.

Ramses II now stands right off of Central Ave., looming far larger than he ever did in front of a 32-story-tall pyramid.

The statue, which is fiber glass, was built in 1991 by special permission of the Egyptian government.

You don't need to be a rocket scientist to know and remember Pharaoh from the Bible. He was a cruel Egyptian ruler whom controlled slaves for his own personal gain and efforts.

So anytime we set up statues for the inappropriate reason or purpose; it can bring havoc to our area. It is forbidden in the Holy Scriptures and one of the great commandments which man shouldn't do.

We are not talking about all statues; but statues and monuments which create hostility and injustice for others.

We should never create, build, or establish a statue in place as a reminder for others to acknowledge who is in authority or in control. How can we forget how this angered God with the Israelites when they

made the golden calf (Exodus 32)? We should all live in harmony so that God will be pleased.

God has given man authority over many things Psalms 8. But God is Supreme Being over All and everything. This is the absolute truth; whether some agree or disagree.

Does this mean we should have divided organizations and civil rights platforms? Well; I think it depends on what the purpose and reason for the organization or entity. We can exercise our rights in a way which aren't offensive to any race or ethnic background.

The Mindset

What was the mindset of the police officer *Darren Wilson* on the day of the shooting? What was the mindset of high school graduate; Michael Brown on that day?

In my opinion; I think fear played a huge factor with them both. Both were tall men, but they were trying to defend their own lives.

Both may have felt that either of them was going to die that day. The facts state many things and we have seen video clippings of more facts.

Do the facts in the convenient store justify the shooting or his actions? It couldn't have. Why? It is because the police officer; Darren Wilson hadn't seen the tapes or video. So we know we can throw this factor out*of*the* window . The report states that the victim was walking in the middle of the road; (which is consistent as "jay walking").

My first thought on this was; this officer didn't wake up from his bed and plotted to kill a black man. I truly don't believe this. Ferguson, Missouri may have past and present issues regarding race; but I don't think this officer intended for this to happen.

This officer was performing his duties and saw an issue which needed correcting and the situation escalated from there. We cannot overlook the facts of a matter. I begin to pray for the officer and his family as well as the victim's family members.

We have always taught our sons whom are adults to always respect the law. I think these immature rap songs have contributed much behaviour of the African American men.

I cannot figure out how the music industry has approved and accepted

all of these music lyrics which illustrate behaviour against law enforcement. As I stated; I have adult sons and they both support rap; but they also know not to disrespect the law.

I think the actions of one or both could have caused this situation to turn out in a different way.

So without the facts; the mindset reflects back to racism. Some will feel injustice at times. Why? It is because some aren't educated with their local laws and government policies.

I cannot imagine how the mother and father felt of their son. With all of the news media and interviews; the two appeared very hurt and needed answers.

I cannot say how I would've reacted, because I haven't been in the situation and will never tell a parent how to handle a situation such as this.

I can say that we can change the mindset in some areas in which we face. So what are you saying? Earlier in this chapter I stated that we refer to race on everything.

Ferguson as alleged can be a city of racism or indifference. But now there is an opportunity to make things better through healing. When? No one knows.

There are mindset wounds and inner emotional wounds which are still surfacing some. Do they have this right? Yes, until they can come to grips in the mindset. They have the right to exercise their grievances and concerns in public. They are hurt and this is their way of voicing their pain.

Years ago it wasn't head of African American exercising anything. They had to take what was dished out to them and button their lips.

But as we can see in the 21st. Century; these rules and behaviours are squashed.

How can we all heal from this? Did you see the words we? When something on this sort of magnitude occurs whether white, black, or Hispanic; it affects us all.

I have sat for days praying and sometimes weeping for others whom have experienced pain and loss in their lives. So if we are citizens of the United States; it will affect you as well.

The United States were born and birthed on just that; UNITY-

UNITED.

How can we change the mindset? We must reframe from using racism as a crutch. I have been guilty of this as well.

Let me share a story with you. I shopped at a department store one day and as I was going through the aisles; I met a Caucasian older lady.

Me being spiritual or a Christian person; I spoke to her and she didn't return a reply.

So the Holy Spirit whispered and said; Go back and speak to her again." I thought this prejudice lady doesn't want to speak to me. She refused to speak to me the first time.

But I obeyed God and went back to speak once again. I said; good morning and she turned around and replied; "Praise the Lord!" Isn't God good?"

She said ma'am "I am thanking God for bringing me through a triple bypass heart surgery and I am alive to tell about it."

My heart dropped to the floor. I felt really dumb; right. Here I was judging her for her race because I thought she didn't speak and here she is showing herself a better person than I was.

All sorts of things came to my mindset. I thought she probably didn't hear me; poor thing.

After that day; I have learned not to judge others due to the expression upon their face. As we all have heard; you can't judge a book by its cover." She probably was feeling some pain from her surgery when I saw the expression on her face.

Can you see where I am going with this? We can judge others due to our mindset and not see the full picture.

I felt bad for thinking those thoughts. This came from my mindset.

I cannot defend one or the other in the Ferguson case, but I do know that there is a long road ahead of them. Why? It is because they have changed many things since the shooting and they are still in chaos.

Their will need to be some wounds which needs healing from this. The wounds will need to be healed on both sides; from the citizens, the family members of *Michael Brown* the police officer (*Darren Wilson*), and the police department.

I do feel strongly that there have been some old policies and practices which have occurred in this town of Ferguson.

 It has gone on for so long and it had to take this young man's' death in order for the "*good old boys*" to shape up.

The people are angry and frustrated; not only because of *Michael Browns'* death. They are angry due to all the injustice which have may have occurred before.

Something has gone on in this town of Ferguson for the madness to be so intense.
Of course no one is talking because they may already know.

The people whether black, Hispanic, or white is expressing how they feel. An African American will become more violent and the situation will become more intensified when there is no communication. All of the facts weren't in as it was stated.

But I wouldn't have allowed this to go on that long without responding to the family. I feel that the former Chief; *Tom Jackson* did a crappy job of handling the case and he should've been more transparent with both sides.

A law enforcement officer shouldn't rectify another one's actions unless all of the facts are in first. The chief; Tom Jackson could've had a chance if he stayed neutral until the facts came in. He immediately defended his officer without viewing all the details.

The officer; *Darren Brown* was vindicated without all of the facts being in and the family was enraged by this. The former chief should have placed himself in the victims' shows and the officers' shoes.

No one knows what goes through the minds of a mother or father whom has lost their child to gun violence.

All we can do is pray for them and see that laws are changed and enforced correctly. Many; as I; have all sorts of solutions of how this should've played out.

But I strongly feel that if this wouldn't have occurred; then Ferguson wouldn't be on the map today.

I mean some things will occur to "shake up some people." I just hate that it had to come to this in order to expose this city or town.

The city of Ferguson will never be forgotten. It will always hold the positions as the "town of racism." They can move past this but it will continue to plague the minds of some.

This town can be repaired, but it will take a moment in order for this to occur. To place a black chief in position to think this will cause the pain to go away was the wrong approach.

The people aren't ignorant. Promotions should have been available to all from the beginning and not after a precious life has been taken.

The people are still angered because of past wounds and hurts from other victims or issues which have occurred. They are not willing for it to rest at this time.

Is this right? It is right as longs as they have the opportunity to exercise their rights.

Breaking the Silence Factor

In our Metropolitan area in the South of Memphis, Tennessee; they have many ways of communicating and relating with communities.

The police director; *Tony Armstrong* do not assign certain officers to certain area. They all must work together in all neighborhoods.

The city of Memphis (Police department) has programs and hospitality services where they check on the elders if the heat is strong and hot.

They also provide food baskets and so much more for the citizens. I have seen on the media that white police officers have visited African American homes and shown so much love and concern in Memphis.

I feel that law enforcement needs more communication with their citizens.

This doesn't mean the officers should be friends or bowl with them.

 But the officers and their communities can come together and make peace.

An old saying years ago states that;

"You can draw more flies with honey than you can with vinegar." A kind word or acts of efforts can go a long way.

You can be nice and firm at the same time. It doesn't remove any stripes from a law enforcement officer to be kind.

I also strongly believe if the former chief of Ferguson would've have communicated with the family; this would've have brought more peace to the parents and friends.

If the truth be told; some races; such as Caucasians have always made up the rules and have felt there was no need to explain anything to anyone.

If someone has died; they have felt that they don't need to explain why.

This has gone on for centuries and still remains in our great country. This is also a mindset issue. No one desires to sit down and discuss the matters at hand.

Everyone wants to play the silent but blame game.

No one desires to apologize for any wrong doings or mishaps.

This is why racism has gone on for so long in America.
There is no communication and some feel that they don't need to communicate.

Many times we turn our heads to the truth or to a situation and feel that the situation will go away.

All to no effect; the situation will grow lumpier. This is why God will allow these things to occur in order for us to work these things out together.

There will be no certain race in Heaven.

The book of Revelation states that they will be coming from all languages, nations, and tongues (Revelations 7:9). So there will be no partiality or racism on that day.

We must communicate in order to resolve these issues. I mentioned in a previous chapter regarding the old

lady whom had the surgery.

I wouldn't have known about her pains and issues unless I went back to communicate with her. If I wouldn't have communicated with her I would have harbored her

expressions ANGRY within in until this very day.

Communication is so essential for us today in all cases.

When we refuse to communicate this will infuse the situation. It doesn't matter if the facts are in or not; just say something.

You or I may not be able to reveal everything; but just say something. The former chief; *Tom Jackson* could have offered an apology for their loss.

This isn't admitting wrong doing; this is just exercising "good home training."

We always offer kindness to a loss, no matter who's at fault. I am no ways of blaming former Chief *Tom Jackson.*

I am not aware of his *"report card"* as a chief. I imagined he was fine officer in many ways. I am just providing some tips on how we can defuse a situation or how he could have defused the matter.

Communication can resolve many entities if we sit down and think the process through. This was an event which I can declare the "turn of the century." I have never seen a protest and outcry as this in all of my days.

There were commentators which interviewed guests on their shows and you could see the tension between the guests and the interviewer.

Some of the guests had necks which turned red and some where you could see their veins in their necks.

It was hilarious at times to view this but painful that we haven't moved very far from this era in our society.

One of our favorite commentators and TV hosts is *Dr. Drew. Dr. Drew* will get to the hard core of the issue and break each situation down.

He will tear the matter a part. He will allow all of his guests a fair response without prejudice.

We love *Dr. Drew* in our home. His shows and segments aren't impartial. But there were some television show hosts whom couldn't hide their feelings and emotions.

The mindset can keep us stifled regarding reality of what is going on around us.

Just as the hit TV sitcom of *Good Times. Good Times* has always been a family show which many have loved.

It depicts a black African American family which is poor living in government assistance housing and

struggling to pay bills.

At the end of the day they still remain happy within themselves as a result of; no one can separate a family which have endured struggles together.

Before the economic crash occurred in 2008; Good Times would play on the television of millions of those whom watched.

I feel that these sorts of shows are displayed to keep the mindset of the African Americans to remain in poverty.

It allows them to feel that they cannot do any better than the projects and low income assistance.

This is a mindset and communicational barrier.

After the economic crash hit; *Good Times* hasn't been seen again. Why?

My opinion is this.
It would allow African Americans to get up and seek a job

and that the government can no longer support them.

 It is amazing how others can communicate with others through media devices and the people aren't aware of it.

It is still a mindset issue. This is the way some find ways to communicate with others through media and not face to face.

I believe in the Republicans motto. Our grandmother would always say; "Every tub should sit on its own bottom."

This means everyone should be self sufficient.

We can erase or overlook the fact of racism in our beautiful country; but racism is still alive today.

The mindset allows some to not forget it and for some to erase it from their minds as if it doesn't exist.

It is due to the communication barrier. African Americans were attacked on every side regarding the death of *Michael Brown*.

The Caucasians were mauled as well due to the mindset of slavery and injustice. They were blamed for the slavery mechanism all over again.

If an African American is mistreated; many of their mindsets will return back to the slavery and racism mentality.

 The Caucasians will always say that it is ignorance. This is true to a certain extent.

If we allow all to feel equal; then I think the mindset will begin to heal and overcome these barriers
 which have crippled our country for so many centuries?

We are all in this together. We should find ways to sit down and discuss which is plaguing our country.

Prejudices can appear on both sides of the fence. This is not a Caucasian prejudice. It is an all racial prejudice. Ferguson can be healed but it will take some time. Working together is just one major success to healing.

About The Author

Diane is a native of Pontiac, Michigan. She is the Ceo of two nonprofit organizations; The Networking Partners, and The National Extraordinary Professional Women. She is also the hosts of three radio shows; The Professional Pastors, Bold Women of Faith, & Women Who Rock with Success. She is the pastor of Saint Petersburg Global Ministries. Mrs. Winbush has written over 100 books in Christianity, Youth, Romance, Relationships, business & Marketing.

www.ingramcontent.com/pod-product-compliance
Lightning Source LLC
Chambersburg PA
CBHW040847180526
45159CB00001B/343